*The affinities of all the beings. . .
have sometimes been represented
by a great tree. . .the great Tree of Life,
which fills with its dead and broken branches
the crust of the earth, and covers the surface
with its ever branching and beautiful ramifications.*

—Charles Darwin, from *On the Origin of Species*

*Keep a green tree in your heart and perhaps a singing bird will come.*

— Chinese proverb

# THE Universe Is a TREE

Laura Filippucci

Creative Editions

# INTRODUCTION

*The clearest way into the Universe*
*is through a forest wilderness.*

—John Muir, from *John of the Mountains:*
*The Unpublished Journals of John Muir*

Our ancestors lived in a world covered in forest. Trees gave early humans shelter, food, and materials for building, making tools, and fuel. Trees were considered powerful, magical beings rooted in the earth that reached skyward to the heavens above. Not only did trees sustain other living things, but they also seemed immortal: Their leaves would fall off and grow back again, and they could sprout new growth, even if burnt or broken. Trees were sacred, and they were respected and worshiped.

The ancient reverence for trees has waned. But we can still marvel at a tree's beauty, be awed by its majesty. Trees still speak to us if we are willing to listen. They speak to us about the importance of caring for the natural world (and of our interconnectedness). So let us be among the trees: This book is a guide through the forest of our imagination, exploring the meaning and importance of a variety of trees from around the world.

## TREES ARE CREATORS
# Redwood

Coast redwood (*Sequoia sempervirens*)
Giant sequoia (*Sequoiadendron giganteum*)

*To be like these, straight, true and fine,*
*to make our world like theirs, a shrine;*
*Sink down, Oh, traveler, on your knees,*
*God stands before you in these trees.*

—Joseph B. Strauss, from "The Redwoods"

Redwoods are ancient trees that once lined the entire Pacific coast of
North America. Native peoples like the Tolowa, the Sinkyone, and the
Yurok used Redwood timber for building their huts and boats, and
the bark, nuts, and leaves for food and medicine. But, out of respect,
they never cut down living trees.

When settlers arrived in the 19th century, they cut the trees down
by the millions to build houses and railroads. By the end of that century,
so little was left of the Redwood forests that the first-ever conserva-
tion associations and national parks were created to protect them.

## TREES ARE ANCESTORS
### *Kauri*
*Agathis australis*

*You are lost to the night,    Shining cuckoo, crying now,*
*O great Kauri lying there.    Fly sadly here, fly sadly here.*

        —Maori wake song

The Kauri is very important to New Zealand's indigenous people, the
Maori. According to legend, in the beginning of time, Heaven, the father,
and Earth, the mother, were clinging together so close that all their children were crushed in the darkness. The god of the forest, Tāne Mahuta,
managed to pull apart his parents, and this gave light to the world. His
eldest son, the first Kauri tree, stood as a pillar to hold up the sky. Kauri's
brother, the First Whale, invited him to go swimming in the sea, but Kauri
could not go because his skin was not waterproof. So Brother Whale gave
him a skin like his own, smooth and oily. That's why Kauri bark is gray,
thin, and waterproof.

## TREES ARE TEMPLES

# *Oak*

English oak (*Quercus robur*)

*But you, you majestic ones, stand like a people of Titans*
*In the tamer world, and you belong only to yourselves and to the heavens*
*that nurtured and raised you, and to the earth that bore you.*

—Friedrich Hölderlin, from "Die Eichbäume" (The Oak Trees),
Translated by Anne MacKinney

For many ancient peoples, the Oak is considered the most sacred of trees. The Celts held their secret rituals in secluded Oak groves. In medieval times, people thought that Oak woods sheltered the secret meetings of fairies and witches, and for the English and German country people, Oaks were home to the Green Man, a mysterious oak-leaf-clad creature who was a magical protector of nature. In Norfolk, England, archaeologists have found a temple older than the famous prehistoric stone circle at Stonehenge: a circle of Oak trunks, with a big upturned tree in its center as an altar.

## TREES ARE HOMES OF THE GODS
# *Cedar of Lebanon*
### *Cedrus libani*

*They beheld the cedar mountain, abode of the gods.*

—from *Epic of Gilgamesh*

In ancient Mesopotamia, the Cedar tree was revered as the home of Enki, the earth god, creator of humankind. Not everyone respected sacred trees as they should have, though. In the *Epic of Gilgamesh*, the hero Gilgamesh finds himself in a sacred grove of Cedars, cuts down the trees, and kills their guardian spirit. He is punished by the gods for his arrogance and forced to endure a series of trials. Humans, too, have threatened the Cedar: In ancient times, this tree grew all over the mountain ranges around the Mediterranean Sea, but for many centuries, its wood was considered the best for building ships, palaces, and temples. Today, very few Cedars are still standing in Lebanon and northern Africa.

## TREES ARE GATES TO THE BEYOND

*Taxus baccata*

*Of vast circumference and gloom profound*
*This solitary tree! a living thing*
*Produced too slowly ever to decay;*
*Of form and aspect too magnificent*
*To be destroyed.*

—William Wordsworth, from "Yew-trees"

Yews were considered magical trees, because they can live for thousands of years, and because they can regenerate from the roots and even from fallen trunks. But they were menacing, too: their leaves and seeds are poisonous. For thousands of years, Yews have been symbolic portals to worlds beyond the grave. The Norse people of northern Europe told stories of Yggdrasil, a huge tree (sometimes described as an Ash) standing in the center of the earth, with its great roots extending to different realms. The gnarled ancient Yews near old churches, planted to mark and protect those holy places long ago, remind us of this connection between the visible and invisible worlds.

## TREES ARE CHANNELS TO OTHER WORLDS
# Kapok
### *Ceiba pentandra*

*Climbing this tree, the serpent becomes bird*
*and the word, song.*

—Pablo Antonio Cuadra, from *The Ceiba Tree*

One of the tallest trees in the world, the Ceiba, or Kapok, towers above the Amazon rainforest. The ancient Maya believed that the whole universe was created and contained by a gigantic Ceiba that stood at the center of the world. Its roots reached the underworld, its trunk contained the middle world where people lived, and its immense crown of branches held up the thirteen levels of the Mayan heaven. Only the spirits and the shamans could travel up and down the tree, between the sky, the earth, and the under-world, using the tree's many branches and vines as highways. Similarly, in the rainforest, the Ceiba hosts a multitude of plants and animals that grow, move, and feed among the huge pillars at its base, its high branches, and its dangling vines.

## TREES ARE GIVERS
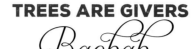
# Baobab
*Adansonia digitata*

*Under the baobab*
*Oft have I slept,*
*Fanned by sweet breezes*
*That over me swept.*

—Anonymous, from "Zaza, the Female Slave"

The mighty Baobab grows in most parts of Africa and is a symbol of this
continent. Legend states that in the beginning of time, the creator assigned
trees to the animals. The hyena was given a Baobab but complained of its
ugliness. Angered, the creator uprooted the tree and threw it back into the
ground upside down. Its shape *is* unusual: Its squat trunk can become very
fat, because it stores water in its spongy wood, and its branches are short
and barren for most of the year, so it looks like an upside-down tree with
roots reaching towards the sky! The Baobab provides food, medicine, water, and precious shade to villagers and their cattle, and shelter and water to
wild animals, travelers, and shepherds in the dry savanna.

# Sweet Chestnut

*Castanea sativa*

*O chestnut tree, great rooted blossomer,*
*Are you the leaf, the blossom or the bole?*
*O body swayed to music, O brightening glance,*
*How can we know the dancer from the dance?*

—William Butler Yeats, from "Among School Children"

There are ancient Chestnut trees all over Europe, but the most famous and possibly the oldest is in Sicily, Italy, on the slopes of Mount Etna. Legend has it that a queen was visiting the famous Sicilian volcano when a sudden storm caught up to her and her retinue of 100 horsemen and women. They all found refuge under a giant Chestnut tree that from then on was called the "Castagno dei Cento Cavalli" (Chestnut of One Hundred Horses). The Castagno still stands today, at an age of more than 2,000 years, and is now protected by the local people and visited as a natural monument.

## TREES ARE BEARERS OF PEACE

*Olive*

*Olea europaea*

*But I am like an olive tree*
*flourishing in the house of God;*
*I trust in God's unfailing love*
*for ever and ever.*

—Psalm 52:8, the New International Version

In Mediterranean lands, the Olive tree was sacred to the ancient Egyptians, the Jews, the Greeks, and the Romans. In the Bible, the Olive tree is a symbol of wisdom and of the alliance with God. The dove sent by Noah from the Ark flies back bearing an olive leaf in its beak, announcing the end of the flood and the renewal of peace between God and humanity (Genesis 8:11). For centuries, holy men, princes, poets, and the winners of contests were crowned with olive wreaths and anointed with olive oil. Today, the Olive tree is still widely grown in many countries around the world for oil and fruits, and it is also loved everywhere as a symbol of peace.

銀杏

## TREES ARE HEALERS
# *Ginkgo*
### *Ginkgo biloba*

*In garments of gold*
*They look like little birdies*
*Dancing in the sky*
*The leaves of the Ginkgo tree*
*Floating down in the late sun.*

—Akiko Yosano

The Ginkgo was the first tree to evolve from prehistoric plants, millions of years before dinosaurs roamed the planet. It has remained unchanged, but today it can be found in the wild only in very remote parts of China. Since ancient times, Ginkgoes were planted near temples and sacred places. In traditional Asian medicine, Gingko leaves, seeds, and fruits were used as remedies against many illnesses, and even modern medicine uses substances obtained from its leaves. Among the few living beings that survived near the epicenter of the blast of the 1945 atomic bomb in Hiroshima are four Ginkgo trees that continue to remind people of the cruelty of war and the resilience and healing power of trees.

# TREES ARE FOUNTS OF WISDOM

# Banyan Bodhi
### Ficus benghalensis Ficus religiosa

*He longed to be the wind and blow through your resting branches,*
*to be your shadow and lengthen with the day on the water,*
*to be a bird and perch on your topmost twig.*

—Rabindranath Tagore, from "The Banyan Tree"

More than 2,000 years ago, Prince Siddhartha sat under a Bodhi to meditate. Eventually, he achieved supreme wisdom and became the Buddha, which means the Enlightened. Two trees descended from this sacred tree, called the Tree of Knowledge, are still alive today and venerated in India and Sri Lanka.

Ancient Indians imagined the Universal Tree, from which all living beings originate, as a Banyan or Bodhi tree. In the Hindu religion, the Banyan hosts the three most powerful gods: Vishnu in its bark, Brahma in its roots, and Shiva in its branches.

## TREES ARE KEEPERS OF SECRETS
# Bristlecone Pine
*Pinus longaeva*

*You say, what is the time waiting for in its spring?*
*I tell you it is waiting for your branch that flows,*
*because you are a sweet-smelling diamond architecture*
*that does not know why it grows.*

— Zackary Scholl, from "For the Bristlecone Snag"

On the windy, rocky slopes of the White Mountains of the Sierra Nevada live the oldest trees in the world. Among these solitary ancients is a tree called Methuselah. At more than 5,000 years old, this Bristlecone pine was a young tree when the pyramids of Egypt were built! By studying the tree-ring patterns of Bristlecones, scientists can learn what the climate was like at different points in time.

Since the air in the Sierra Nevada is very dry, Bristlecone pines can stand for thousands of years, even long after they are dead, gnarly ghosts guarding their remote kingdom.

## QUOTES ABOUT TREES

*Trees are the earth's endless effort to speak to the listening heaven.*
—Rabindranath Tagore

*Trees are sanctuaries. Whoever knows how to speak to them, whoever knows how to listen to them, can learn the truth.*
*They do not preach learning and precepts, they preach, undeterred by particulars, the ancient law of life.*
—Hermann Hesse

*I took a walk in the woods and came out taller than the trees.*
—Henry David Thoreau

*Trees are poems that earth writes upon the sky.*
—Kahlil Gibran

*You will find something far greater in the woods than in books.*
—Saint Bernard of Clairvaux

*And this, our life, exempt from public haunt, finds tongues in trees, books in the running brooks, sermons in stones, and good in everything.*
—William Shakespeare

*We all travel the Milky Way together, trees and men.*
—John Muir

# SOURCES

Hageneder, Fred. *The Meaning of Trees: Botany, History, Healing, Lore.* San Francisco: Chronicle Books, 2005.

Hight, Julian. *Britain's Tree Story: The History and Legends of Britain's Ancient Trees.* Swindon, UK: National Trust, 2012.

Lewington, Anna, and Edward Parker. *Ancient Trees: Trees That Live for 1,000 Years.* New York: Sterling, 1999.

Pakenham, Thomas. *Remarkable Trees of the World.* New York: W. W. Norton, 2002.

Rival, Laura, ed. *The Social Life of Trees: Anthropological Perspectives on Tree Symbolism.* New York: Berg, 1998.

Text and illustrations copyright © 2018 by Laura Filippucci
Edited by Kate Riggs; Designed by Rita Marshall, with Laura Filippucci
Published in 2018 by Creative Editions
P.O. Box 227, Mankato, MN 56002 USA
Creative Editions is an imprint of The Creative Company
www.thecreativecompany.us
**Library of Congress Cataloging-in-Publication Data**
Names: Filippucci, Laura, author, illustrator.
Title: The universe is a tree / by Laura Filippucci.
Includes bibliographical references.
Summary: This collection of stories, proverbs, and poems about
trees from around the world reveals that a tree's roots not only
go down deep into the earth, but its branches also reach up and
out into the universe, connecting us all.
Identifiers: LCCN 2017048936 / ISBN 978-1-56846-304-9
Subjects: LCSH: Trees—Juvenile literature.
Classification: LCC QK475.8.F55 2018          DDC 582.16—dc23
First edition 9 8 7 6 5 4 3 2 1

Rooted above, with branches below,
is this immemorial Tree.
It is that bright one, that Eternal;
it is called the immortal.
In it all the worlds rest;
nor does any go beyond it. . .
All that the universe is, moves in life,
emanated from it.

—from *Katha Upanishad*